S0-BYB-926

Your Future as a

POLICE OFFICER

HIGH-DEMAND CAREERS™

Your Future as a
POLICE
OFFICER

RACHEL GIVEN-WILSON AND STEPHANIE WATSON

New York

Published in 2020 by The Rosen Publishing Group, Inc.
29 East 21st Street, New York, NY 10010

Copyright © 2020 by The Rosen Publishing Group, Inc.

First Edition

All rights reserved. No part of this book may be reproduced in any form
without permission in writing from the publisher, except by a reviewer.

Library of Congress Cataloging-in-Publication Data

Names: Given–Wilson, Rachel, author. | Watson, Stephanie, author.
Title: Your future as a police officer / Rachel Given–Wilson and Stephanie Watson.
Description: First edition. | New York, NY : The Rosen Publishing
Group, Inc., 2020. | Series: High–demand careers | Includes
bibliographical references and index. | Audience: Grades 7–12.
Identifiers: ISBN 9781508187929 (library bound) | ISBN 9781508187912 (pbk.)
Subjects: LCSH: Police—Vocational guidance—Juvenile literature. |
Law enforcement—Vocational guidance—Juvenile literature.
Classification: LCC HV7922.G528 2020 | DDC 363.2023—dc23

Manufactured in China

Contents

The work of a police officer involves protecting lives and property. Whether they work as uniformed patrol officers, criminal investigators, traffic officers, or federal agents, police officers must be committed to serving and protecting the people and upholding the laws of the country. Depending on their position, police officers may respond to emergency calls, patrol specific areas, obtain warrants and arrest suspects, collect evidence from crime scenes, write reports and fill out forms, and testify in court.

Detective Suzie Ivy is a criminal investigator in a small town in Arizona. She wanted to be a police officer all her life and finds the job extremely rewarding. She believes that her most important strength as a police officer is compassion, and she tries to use it in her work every day.

There are a number of ways to serve as a police officer. Some police officers wear uniforms and patrol neighborhoods, giving tickets to people who are breaking the law.

"I'm now a detective and my goal is getting people to talk to me. I treat them fairly, keep my word, and never talk down to anyone. This doesn't mean I'm weak or that I can't be aggressive when necessary, but it does mean people trust me and tell me things they wouldn't say to other cops," Ivy said in an interview on HowtoBecomeaPoliceOfficer.com.

Ivy advises aspiring police officers to remember that they are part of a team and know when to ask for help from fellow officers and supervisors. "Police officers go through extreme stress day in and day out while on shift.

Know your weaknesses. You will see humanity at its worst. Always be at your best."

Being a police officer can be a very rewarding job for the right person. However, it is also a demanding and sometimes dangerous career that comes with serious responsibilities. Police officers put themselves in danger in the line of duty. Many officers carry guns and Tasers, which comes with another level of responsibility—the responsibility to avoid hurting people, even when you are afraid for your own safety.

"Police have two rights that even the president does not have, the right to take liberty and to take life," retired police officer Eric L. Adams said in an interview with NPR's Terri Gross. "Those are dear to America. And we must ensure that the highest level of scrutiny and standard goes to anyone who is given that right. […] If you're going to wear this uniform and this badge, you must be of the highest quality."

If you're interested in a career as a police officer, there are plenty of career paths to choose from at the city, state, and federal level. The future outlook for police officers is promising, so now is a great time to be starting to plan your career in the police force!

Chapter 1

WHAT DOES IT TAKE TO BE A POLICE OFFICER?

*P*olice officers enforce laws to protect people and their property. Jobs in law enforcement include uniformed patrol officers, criminal investigators, agents with the Federal Bureau of Investigation (FBI), and more. The responsibilities of these positions vary from job to job and from place to place. Police officers often have to work at a desk, filling out paperwork, because it's important to keep track of every investigation. Sometimes these records are used as evidence in court cases. Police officers may have to testify in court and describe what took place during a robbery, murder, or other crime.

Like many jobs, the work of a police officer involves a lot of paperwork. Police officers have to keep detailed records of all the cases they are working on.

Many officers wear uniforms and badges to show their positions. Some states require their officers to wear protective body armor, also called bulletproof vests. Officers often carry a gun and other equipment, such as handcuffs, a baton, or a Taser.

MAIN RESPONSIBILITIES OF A POLICE OFFICER

A police officer's job varies from day to day and from department to department. As officers gain more experience, their roles also can change. The following are just a few of the tasks that the members of a police department might perform on an average day:

WHAT DOES IT TAKE TO BE A POLICE OFFICER?

Patrol neighborhoods. Officers travel through their beat, the area they are assigned to patrol, by car, motorcycle, bicycle, or on foot. Patrolling gives local law enforcement officers a chance to get to know the people who live in their area, and it helps local residents learn to trust the officers. Becoming familiar with a community can help the police spot suspicious activity when it does occur. Officers patrol alone or with partners. While on patrol, they may have to pursue and arrest people who are breaking the law.

When police officers arrest suspects, they usually handcuff them and take them in a car to the police precinct for further questioning.

Arrest criminals. Often, dispatchers will call officers to the scene of a bank robbery, burglary, assault, or other crime. The officers may have to pursue suspects on foot or by car, and they may have to use force to catch them. Once suspects have been caught and arrested, the officer frisks them to make sure they are not carrying any weapons or drugs. The officer reads them their legal rights (called *Miranda* rights, which begin with the words, "You have the right to remain silent") and transports them to a facility where they are booked for the crime.

Investigate crimes. To investigate a crime, police officers must visit the crime scene, interview witnesses, and collect the evidence (material objects such as fingerprints and hair) that they need to solve the case.

Write reports. Police officers have to keep very detailed reports of the crimes they investigate. They may have to present these reports as evidence during a trial.

Enforce traffic laws. Police officers patrol highways and local roads to catch people who violate traffic laws by speeding or running traffic lights. They give out traffic tickets and citations to motorists who break the law, including those who commit vehicle violations and who are suspected of driving while under the influence of alcohol or drugs. Police officers also direct traffic when there is a car accident, a broken traffic light, or a major event like a concert or demonstration. They might also have to reroute traffic when there is an emergency, such as a flood, downed power line, or other safety hazard. A police officer arriving at the scene of a car accident may have to administer first aid to an injured person until an ambulance arrives.

Some of the other duties a police officer might have to perform include the following:

- Check a warehouse or office building at night to make sure it is secure.
- Settle a domestic dispute.
- Deliver a baby.
- Report potholes, broken traffic lights, or other potentially dangerous road conditions.
- Search for a missing person.
- Recover stolen property.
- Conduct a criminal background check.
- Watch a person or location (conduct surveillance) for suspicious or unlawful activity.
- Assist emergency medical crews or stranded motorists.
- Evacuate people from dangerous situations.
- Issue parking tickets.
- Maintain a patrol car and weapons.

Police officers deal with the daily concerns of people in the community, encourage crime prevention efforts, and strive to preserve the peace.

HIGH SCHOOL AND COLLEGE COURSES

High schools usually don't have police officer programs, but many high school classes offer good preparation for the field. Physical education (PE), Spanish or another foreign language, English, and math all provide useful skills for this career path. A few high schools offer a four-year program in domestic security to help students prepare

Most high schools don't offer police officer programs, but there are a number of classes you can take to prepare for a career in the police force, including Spanish classes.

for careers in homeland security. Besides the standard high school classes, students in such programs can take courses on topics that include nuclear arms, cybercrimes, and domestic militias. Some high schools offer classes in forensic science and law enforcement. These courses provide students with entry-level skills in crime scene photography, evidence collection, fingerprinting, analysis of tool patterns, theories of crime and punishment, ethical practices, search and seizure, gang awareness, patrol tactics, and legal and moral issues.

Many junior colleges, colleges, and universities offer degrees in law enforcement. A background in political science, computer science, law, psychology, sociology, or criminal justice also can be a plus in this field. Majoring in a foreign language, particularly Spanish, is helpful, especially for officers working in areas where there are large populations of Spanish-speaking residents. Participating in the Reserve Officers' Training Corps (ROTC) or another military program can teach the skills necessary for the job, including the use of firearms. Military veterans are given an advantage over other applicants when they apply for police positions.

Police Officers of Color: Finding Community and Making Change

Some police departments have a tense relationship with many communities of color. Several high-profile incidents of police officers killing unarmed black men, women, and children have drawn attention to a culture of racism within many police departments. For people of color who want to join the police force, this can be a difficult situation to navigate. There are a number of organizations that exist to provide support and community for police officers of color. These include the National Association of Black Police Officers, Blacks in Law Enforcement of America, and the National Black Police Association.

Retired New York Police Department (NYPD) Captain Eric L. Adams joined the police force because he wanted to change the culture of the police force from within. In a 2014 op-ed in the *New York Times*, Adams described how he experienced violence at the hands of police officers as

(continued on the next page)

(continued from the previous page)

a fifteen-year-old black boy in Jamaica, Queens, in New York City. He had tried to put this moment behind him, but every time he heard a new story about police violence against people of color, he was reminded of the injustice he had suffered. Eventually, Adams decided to join the police force. "I didn't want any more children to go through what I endured, so I sought to make change by joining the police department."

Adams found it disturbing that his fellow officers "started their shift on the defensive, thinking about protecting themselves, as opposed to the communities they served, regardless of the complexion of those communities." Adams founded the advocacy group 100 Blacks in Law Enforcement Who Care, a group of police officers who work to improve relations between the NYPD and communities of color. Many other police officers across the country are working hard to improve police relations with communities of color.

PERSONAL QUALIFICATIONS

Applicants for a job as a police officer must be US citizens. They usually have to be at least twenty-one years old. However, some police departments hire eighteen-year-olds as cadets or interns and then train them in basic police skills for a couple of years. Once they turn twenty-one, the cadets or interns may be considered for a position in the regular police force. (Some states and counties will allow trainees to become officers at a younger age.)

Because it is a police officer's job to uphold the law, applicants cannot have had any felony convictions. (Background checks will confirm this, so it is important to be truthful on applications and in interviews.) People who have domestic violence convictions or have used drugs recently cannot become law enforcement officers. They also must never have been fired from a job for poor behavior or have received a dishonorable discharge from the US military. Young people with goals of becoming a police officer should have a good driving history and manage their money wisely. Prospective employers will look closely at candidates' financial backgrounds to ensure that their applicants are responsible citizens.

The best law enforcement officers are honest, trustworthy, intelligent, and have good leadership abilities and excellent judgment. They are emotionally stable— they are able to control their anger and emotions in even the most dangerous situations. Officers also need to be healthy and strong enough to handle the tough physical demands of the job. People who meet these requirements and are up to the challenges of being a police officer can start looking for open positions in a police department in their region.

Chapter 2

TRAINING TO BECOME A POLICE OFFICER

Police officers don't need to have a college degree to work for state and local police departments, but they do need to pass a written and physical police exam and undergo a thorough background check. Once they are hired for a position, they must complete training at a police academy.

Law enforcement provides plenty of room for advancement for talented, hardworking officers. Officers usually become eligible for promotion after a probationary period. Some officers move up to detective or begin specializing in one area.

PASSING THE POLICE EXAM

When a police force is hiring, it will post an announcement that it is holding a police exam. People who are interested in a job can fill out an application, which includes a list of questions about their education, past employment experience, and other personal information. If they meet the basic qualifications for the police department, they will be invited to take the written exam—the first step in the police application process.

Applicants must pass the written exam before they can even be considered for a job. The written exam ensures that applicants are able to understand materials, such as laws and handbooks, and communicate effectively. It also tells whether or not applicants can respond appropriately to the types of situations they would encounter while on the police force. The higher an applicant's score, the faster that person is considered for an open position. Candidates who fail the written test the first time may be allowed to take it again at a later time.

Most tests include multiple-choice questions, but a few require applicants to answer written questions about a scene they watch in a video or write an original passage that shows their reasoning and writing skills. Questions usually include the following: reading comprehension (to see how well the applicant understands information presented in a passage and makes decisions based on that information), basic math (addition, subtraction, multiplication, and division), memory, grammar and spelling, and map reading.

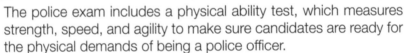

The police exam includes a physical ability test, which measures strength, speed, and agility to make sure candidates are ready for the physical demands of being a police officer.

Candidates who pass the written test will also need to take a physical ability test to make sure they can handle the physical demands of the job. This test measures speed, strength, and agility. It may involve challenges like running, doing sit-ups and push-ups, and completing obstacle courses. A standard fitness test may involve the following tasks:

¤ Run up and down a flight of stairs.
¤ Push a 100-pound (45-kilogram) sandbag about 15 feet (4.5 meters) and return it to its original position.

☼ Climb a fence that is 6 feet (2 m) high.
☼ Drag a 160-pound (72 kg) dummy for 30 feet (9 m).
☼ Load and fire a weapon.
☼ Get through a narrow window.
☼ Walk across a beam that is 12 feet (3.6 m) in length.
☼ Run 500 feet (152 m) to the finish line.

Finally, candidates have to pass a medical exam. A doctor measures the person's blood pressure, height, weight, and heart function. Hearing, vision, and strength are also tested. Candidates may have to give blood and urine samples so that they can be tested for potential health problems, such as high cholesterol. A sample of the person's urine will probably be tested for traces of drugs. Any serious medical condition or evidence of illegal drug use can be enough reason for a candidate to be rejected. Even color blindness or being overweight can disqualify someone from joining the police force.

PERSONAL HISTORY, INTERVIEWS, AND BACKGROUND CHECKS

Knowing that a person can meet the physical and mental demands of the police force is not enough. An officer must also be honest and emotionally stable. To determine these qualities, the police department will first take a personal history. That personal history can be as long as thirty pages, and it might include questions such as the following:

☼ Where were you born?
☼ Where did you go to school?

¤ Where did you work?

¤ To what organizations did you belong?

The police department will confirm the information on these documents through a background investigation, criminal history check, and possibly a lie detector test. During the background check, an investigator may call the applicant's friends, relatives, neighbors, and coworkers and check public and private records to make sure that everything the person has said is true. The background investigation will include many important details of the applicant's life. Some of the information provided may be very personal or embarrassing, such as a history of the person's marriage, drug use, and legal problems. During the lie detector test, the applicant is connected to a machine that can supposedly determine whether a statement is true or false. The machine measures any changes in heart rate, breathing rate, and blood pressure that might occur when someone is nervous.

The application process might also include several other tests. These tests can involve a written psychological evaluation and an interview with a psychologist to determine if the person is mentally stable enough to be a police officer. The candidate might also be asked to participate in an oral board interview. During this interview, a panel of commissioners, police personnel, or psychologists asks the person questions about different situations to determine if he or she has the knowledge, communication skills, integrity, and motivation needed to perform the job.

 At the police academy, officers do role playing exercises to practice the skills they will need to use on the force. This includes learning how to deal with violent situations.

POLICE ACADEMY

Once someone is hired by a police force, he or she must go through training at a police academy. Many large local and state police forces have their own police academies. Smaller departments will send their recruits to train at a state or regional academy.

At the police academy, new recruits learn how to become successful police officers. Some recruits live at the academy while they train (this is especially true of federal law enforcement agencies). Other recruits commute from home daily. Trainees may remain at the academy for a few weeks or several months.

Officers must understand the laws and rules of the job by taking a variety of college-style classes on related subjects, including the following:

- Arrest, search, and seizure procedures
- Use of firearms and deadly force
- Criminal and constitutional laws
- Civil rights
- State laws and local ordinances
- Writing citations (such as for traffic violations)
- Conducting interviews and interrogations
- Community relations
- Booking procedures for arrested suspects
- Handling evidence
- Writing reports
- Motor vehicle codes and traffic control
- Accident investigation
- Pursuit driving and other vehicle operations
- Use of warrants
- Police ethics and the Law Enforcement Code of Conduct
- Court procedures and testimony
- First-aid training
- Emergency response
- Crowd control
- Surveillance
- Defense tactics (such as handcuffing, self-defense, and search procedures)

Lieutenant Captain Sample Examination

Police civil service exams require test takers to apply their knowledge of the law and law enforcement procedures. The following are sample exam questions from the Lieutenant/ Captain Examination provided by the Police Tutorial Service.

1. After a search of the Orpheus Theater was conducted and no bomb or other device was found, Sergeant Connolly informed the theater manager that the building was safe for occupancy. In this instance, Sergeant Connolly's action was:

a. proper, as the superior officer at the scene of such an occurrence must be decisive and forceful
b. improper, as Sergeant Connolly has no immediate or supervisory control of the manager of a commercial establishment
c. proper, as cooperation between the police and legitimate businesspeople is a highly recommended objective
d. improper, as such a procedure might involve liability for the department in the event that persons reoccupying the theater are injured or killed from the explosion of a bomb that was not found *(correct answer)*

(continued on the next page)

(continued from the previous page)

2. If a threat is made against a business establishment, a public building, such as a school, an office complex, or warehouse, that a hidden bomb is to be exploded, the decision as to whether the occupants should be evacuated is generally made by:

a. the police officers first at the scene
b. the first superior officer arriving at the scene
c. the first superior of the specialized unit arriving at the scene, such as the bomb squad representative
d. the person in charge of the premises *(correct answer)*

Learning these skills in a classroom is important, but it's also vital for trainees to practice these skills for real so that they are prepared once they enter the police force. At police academy, recruits do role playing exercises in which they act out various scenarios as if they were actually working on the force.

To improve recruits' strength, endurance, and flexibility, the police academy also offers physical training courses that are as grueling as military basic training. Classes usually start by exercising as a group. Then each recruit performs many sets of push-ups, sit-ups, abdominal crunches, pull-ups, and a variety of other exercises. As part of self-defense training, recruits have to learn how to fight—and defend—themselves. This training may involve punching boxing bags, practicing street-fighting techniques (and weapon disarming), learning how to fall, and working with a police baton or Taser. Recruits may practice these techniques hundreds or even thousands of times before they get them right. They will also learn how to take apart firearms, clean them, and reassemble them. They practice shooting firearms over and over again in a variety of ways (such as while kneeling or lying on the ground) until using a weapon becomes second nature.

After graduating from a police academy, officers receive their police badge and certifications (in areas such as cardiopulmonary resuscitation [CPR], speed enforcement, or weapons) and a position with the police department to which they applied. Their training, however, does not end once they graduate from the police academy. For the first few months on the force, new officers, also known as rookies, are assigned to an experienced field training officer (FTO), who guides them and keeps track of their progress. The FTO evaluates the officers' performance for one year to eighteen months. Any new officers who do not meet the department's standards are let go. Those who make it through the probation period become officers.

MOVING UP THROUGH THE RANKS

Officers can become eligible for promotion after about three to five years. They may become a detective, specialize in a particular area of law enforcement (such as drug enforcement), or get promoted in rank

 There are many opportunities for promotion within the police force. Some officers go on to become corporals, sergeants, lieutenants, or police chiefs

to corporal, sergeant, lieutenant, and, finally, captain or chief of police. Whether officers qualify for a promotion is based on their written exam scores and job performance.

Officers can improve their performance by continuing their education at local colleges, police department academies, or federal agency training centers. The higher the rank of an officer, the more education is required for that position. For example, a sergeant may need only a two-year college degree, whereas a captain will likely have a four-year college degree. Getting additional training also helps officers to stay on top of the latest law enforcement techniques and equipment. Some police departments will pay for their officers to complete their college education or obtain an advanced degree.

Chapter 3

UNIFORMED AND PATROL OFFICERS

*P*olice officers may work for local, state, or federal law enforcement departments. The educational requirements for local police departments are usually less strict than those for federal departments. To get a job with a city police department, a person may need only a high school diploma or general equivalency diploma, whereas a state patrol officer will usually need a college degree.

Uniformed police officers can get hired with just a high school diploma and a year or two of related work experience (for example, working in security or the corrections system). Some police departments, however, require that candidates have completed a year or more

Patrol officers usually wear uniforms and are assigned to patrol a specific neighborhood. They may be called on to assist with all kinds of situations, including settling disputes.

Officers work in police departments of different sizes, from small rural communities to big cities. Municipal (urban) police officers work within the city limits. County officers cover the areas outside cities. In small departments, officers may handle various jobs, from patrolling the streets to writing reports. Larger departments typically assign officers to a specific duty.

PATROL OFFICERS

Patrol officers are the public face of the police department. When someone calls 911 to report a burglary, murder, accident, or other emergency situation, patrol officers are sent to the scene. Patrol officers also drive through cities at night, looking for people who are acting suspiciously. If a crime is being committed, the officer may have to pursue and arrest suspects. However, the life of a patrol officer isn't all about high-speed car chases and thrilling criminal cases. Officers may be called in to assist with all kinds of situations, from settling a domestic dispute to getting a cat out of a tree.

Patrol officers must be good problem solvers, able to think on their feet no matter how unexpected the situation might be. They must have a good understanding of local laws and ordinances so that they know how to respond to various incidents. Moreover, patrol officers can never lose their cool. They must always remain calm under pressure.

TRAFFIC OFFICERS

Traffic officers are uniformed officers who patrol the roads and highways of every town, city, and state, enforcing

Traffic officers patrol roads and highways, looking out for people who are driving over the speed limit or under the influence of alcohol or illegal substances.

traffic laws. Traffic officers may be found parked by the side of a highway using a radar gun to catch speeders. Once they catch someone, they will check the person's license and registration and issue a ticket. Traffic officers also perform routine vehicle checks, looking for drivers who have been drinking or taking illegal drugs or who may have committed a crime. Sometimes a traffic officer will have to arrest a driver who is breaking the law.

Traffic officers also may be found at the scene of an accident. They will help people who were injured in the crash, call for an ambulance, and direct traffic around the accident. Officers often investigate the cause of accidents, and they may have to report what they find in court. Sometimes traffic officers spend their days monitoring parking meters and issuing tickets to cars that are parked at expired meters.

Traffic officers need only a high school diploma or its equivalent. In addition, they must have a year of experience working in a public agency or security job or serving in the US military. Because they spend a lot of time in a patrol car, traffic officers must have a valid driver's license.

TRANSIT AUTHORITY OFFICERS

Transit authority officers are assigned to patrol the subway in a big city. During a shift, officers walk through subway stations, watching for illegal activity. They may investigate a suspicious package, clear the station of panhandlers, or catch someone who has stolen a subway rider's wallet or purse.

K-9 OFFICERS AND MOUNTED POLICE

K-9 and mounted police officers have many of the same responsibilities as other uniformed officers. Instead of having another officer as a partner, though, they have a dog or a horse. K-9 officers work with dogs that are specially trained to sniff out bombs or drugs, search for people who are lost or who have committed a crime, and control crowds. Many large city police departments have their own K-9 units.

K-9 officers may be found in many different working situations and surroundings, including airports, seaports, and US borders. At the airport, they may search incoming luggage for illegal substances. At the borders, a trained K-9 team can catch people who are trying to enter the country illegally. At the scene of a building collapse, a K-9 team may be called in to help find victims who are buried underneath the rubble.

In a K-9 unit, both the dog and the officer (called a handler) require special training. The officer learns how to work as a team with his or her canine partner, as well as how to care for the dog. The dog learns skills such as obedience, pursuit, and how to track a scent.

In mounted police units, it is common for police officers and their horses to be involved in crowd control because it's much easier to pass through a crowd on a horse than in a police car. In Canada, the Royal Mounted Police serve as the country's police force. They have been in existence since 1873, and they're recognized by their distinctive red uniforms and ranger hats.

Becoming a mounted police officer requires a lot of training and a commitment to hard work. Trainees are usually seasoned police officers. Training can last from fourteen to twenty weeks, depending on the police department. Mounted police officers not only have to learn how to ride their horses extremely well—often in crowded situations—but they also have to feed and care for their horses and even clean their stalls.

Career Advice from a K-9 Officer

Bruce has been a K-9 officer in the Pensacola Police Department for about ten years. He spends about forty hours a week at work, but he spends twenty-four hours a day with his dog, who even sleeps in his bed! "As a K-9 officer, you're not only responsible for the feeding and care of the K-9, you're responsible for his medical health as well," Bruce said in an interview for Dr. Kit Career Videos.

The work that Bruce and his K-9 do includes narcotics searches, tracking people, and apprehending suspects. "If there's a felony suspect who refuses to surrender, the K-9 will go in and apprehend that suspect or bite him and hold him until the other officers can go in and put him in handcuffs."

K-9 officers have to go through four hundred hours of school with the K-9 they are going to work with. They are then certified to work with that specific dog, as a team. K-9s have a working life of five to seven years. After that, if

K-9 officers often work at airports. Their dogs are trained to sniff out bombs or drugs. K-9 officers go through a rigorous training process with their dogs so they can work together as a team.

the officer wants to continue being a K-9 officer, he or she has to go through another four hundred hours of school with a new dog.

Bruce warns aspiring K-9 officers that the job is hard work—K-9 officers have to be constantly training their dogs, and every time they train them, they have to fill out paperwork.

For Bruce, that additional work is worth it. "[Dogs are] very loyal. They will give their life for you without even thinking about it. In some ways, that is a stress reliever for me because I can always count on the fact that my partner's with me, and that no matter what, if there's some sort of a situation that's dangerous, he's always going to be there to protect me."

SHERIFFS

Sheriffs perform jobs similar to those of uniformed local or county police chiefs. They are in charge of enforcing the laws in their county. Most sheriffs' departments are small, with fewer than twenty-five officers.

Sheriffs conduct criminal investigations. They also arrest people who are breaking the law and process them through the court system and county jail. Sheriffs perform other general law enforcement tasks. A sheriff is often

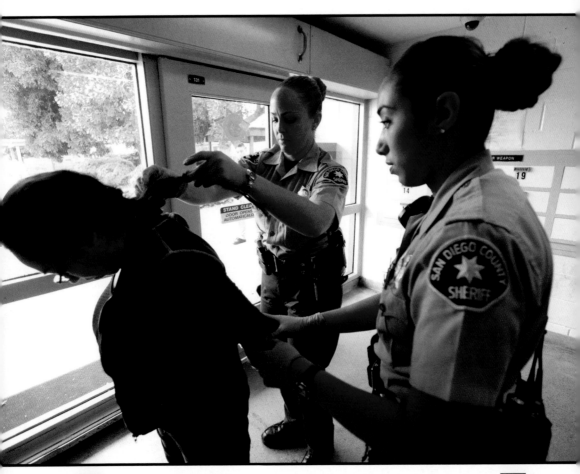

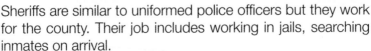

Sheriffs are similar to uniformed police officers but they work for the county. Their job includes working in jails, searching inmates on arrival.

the highest law enforcement position in a county and is usually elected to the position. The sheriff's department may have deputy sheriffs to help transport prisoners or provide security in courtrooms. Requirements for this job are similar to those for a police officer. Applicants usually have to be at least twenty-one years old, a US citizen, and have a high school diploma or its equivalent, and they must go through the police academy or a similar training program.

STATE POLICE

State police officers, sometimes also called state troopers, carry out many of the same functions as local police officers do, but they work for their state, rather than for a city or county within the state. Depending on the state, some of the jobs that state police officers may perform include making arrests, investigating crimes, providing emergency assistance at the scene of a traffic accident, patrolling state highways, and searching people or property for illegal or stolen goods.

To become a state police officer, applicants must have a college degree. They then must complete training at the state police academy.

Chapter 4

DETECTIVES AND CRIMINAL INVESTIGATORS

Not all police officers patrol the streets. Some work as detectives or criminal investigators and work behind the scenes, gathering and examining evidence to solve crimes. These officers typically do not wear uniforms. They may specialize in one area of law enforcement, such as arson, burglary, murder, drugs, organized crime, forgery, gang activity, identity theft, computer forensics, gambling, or financial crimes.

DETECTIVES

When a crime is committed, a uniformed police officer is usually the first person on the scene. The officer questions witnesses, gathers whatever evidence he or she can find,

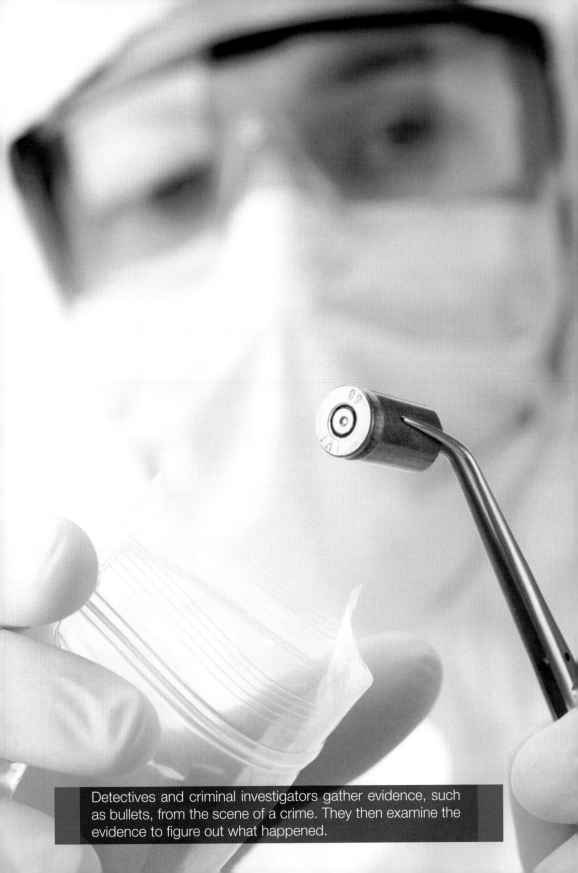

Detectives and criminal investigators gather evidence, such as bullets, from the scene of a crime. They then examine the evidence to figure out what happened.

and arrests the perpetrator. If the crime remains unsolved, one or more detectives are assigned to the case.

Detectives are problem solvers. They investigate crime scenes, looking for the tiniest details to help them determine when the crime occurred, where it occurred, what happened, and what the criminal's motive might have been. To answer these questions, detectives have to search the scene and gather evidence, such as fingerprints, photographs, bullet fragments, hair, and skin.

These pieces of evidence are sent to a crime laboratory. At the lab, technicians use computers to match the evidence with fingerprints and other information from

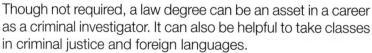

Though not required, a law degree can be an asset in a career as a criminal investigator. It can also be helpful to take classes in criminal justice and foreign languages.

known criminals. During the investigation, detectives also interview people on and around the scene of the crime, including uniformed police officers, victims, witnesses, and possible suspects. Sometimes detectives will use legal surveillance techniques, listening in on suspects' phone conversations or following them around to monitor their activities.

After the detective has collected all possible evidence in a case, he or she will write a report of the crime and submit it to a superior officer. Based on the available evidence, that officer may decide to arrest a suspect (or suspects). The evidence may be used in court during the criminal trial.

Police departments and private companies both hire detectives. Although a college degree is not required, some police departments expect their detectives to have at least a year or two of college. Classes in criminal justice, law, and foreign languages all can be assets in this field. Many detectives start out as police officers. After working as a uniformed officer for several months to a few years and passing a series of tests, candidates may be considered for the position of detective.

Career Advice from Detective Suzie Ivy

Suzie Ivy always wanted to be a police officer, but she didn't become one until she was in her forties. "My school counselor told me there were other careers females were more suited for. It took me thirty years but I finally proved

(continued on the next page)

(continued from the previous page)

him wrong," she said in an interview with Defrosting Cold Cases. Ivy now works as a sex crimes investigator in a small town in Arizona, and she is the author of a number of humorous books including *Bad Luck Cadet* and *Bad Luck Officer*. In an interview on the website How to Become a Police Officer, Ivy shared a story that changed the way she looks at police work:

> I was told that victims of domestic violence go back repeatedly to their abusers and to harden my heart. [...] A single case changed my outlook. [In this case,] the suspect beat his wife in front of their young children. She'd put up with it for years. [...] I took her statement and then made phone calls to find a safe place for her and her children. Before I left, she said, "I don't want to go back to him." [...] I gave her my business card and wrote down my personal cell number. I told her she could call me anytime. She did. She also used me as a reference when she went to the academy for the department of corrections. She's a supervisor today, and she never went back to her abuser. As an officer, never forget your humanity and never give up hope.

OTHER JOBS IN LAW ENFORCEMENT

There are plenty of other careers available for people who enjoy law enforcement but who don't want to become uniformed officers. They include the following jobs:

¤ Crime prevention officer, who teaches crime prevention methods to businesses and schools

- Fugitive search officer, who finds and brings to justice people who have committed a crime and have run from the law
- Fish and game warden, who makes sure that hunters and fishermen are following the law
- Harbor patrol officer, who rescues ships and people who are in danger or distress and finds and arrests criminals who use the waterways
- Hostage negotiation officer, who rescues people who are being held hostage
- Juvenile officer, who protects children who are the victims of abuse or neglect, finds lost or runaway children, and takes into custody children who commit crimes
- Special weapons and tactics (SWAT) officer, who assists police officers during emergency situations, such as riots or hostage standoffs
- Vice officer, who finds and arrests people who are involved in illegal activities related to drugs, gambling, or sex
- Bomb squad officer, who responds to bomb threats and uses robots and trained dogs to find and disarm explosives

Criminal investigators visit the scenes of crimes and interview witnesses about what they saw and heard. They may also call these witnesses in for further questioning at a later date.

Every police department needs a variety of people to support the work of its uniformed officers. Employees working in recruitment, accounting, employee services, public relations, data collecting and reporting, transportation, and the crime laboratory are crucial to the efforts of the police department.

WORKING WITH LGBTQ COMMUNITIES

Brian Sharp is a veteran police officer in the Atlanta Police Department (APD) who conducts trainings with police officers about working with lesbian, gay, bisexual, transgender, and queer (LGBTQ) communities. A gay man, Sharp decided to start doing these trainings when he realized that police interactions with LGBTQ communities were often fraught and that few police departments across the country provided any kind of LGBTQ-awareness training.

"When officers are out on their own patrol and they're dealing with folks, and they come into contact with a group of trans women walking down the street at 2 or 3 o'clock in the morning, they may assume that those people are sex workers, and they use that as probable cause to stop and detain, and maybe ultimately to arrest them," Sharp said in a 2015 interview with *Newsweek*. "One of the things that's covered in the training is that trans people are just like we are: Although some people may be involved in criminal activity, the mere fact of their gender identity does not make them a criminal in itself."

Sharp's program soon caught on and he started getting calls from police departments around the country, asking him to facilitate trainings for them. This type of training is useful for many aspects of a police officer's work. For example, in a routine traffic stop, if someone's gender presentation doesn't match the name on their license, some officers may feel confused or even threatened. "If a person is presenting as a female, you address them as 'ma'am' or 'miss,'" Sharp explains. "I think that's one of the most confusing things a police officer deals with— when somebody is trans and going through transition and wherever they're at in the transition, a police officer has to meet them there."

A 2015 study by the Urban Institute revealed that LGBTQ youth are particularly likely to have negative encounters with law enforcement. Over 70 percent of the 283 young people surveyed for the study said they had been arrested at least once, often for misdemeanor crimes such as fare evasion, and 49 percent of those felt unsafe or had experienced violence at the hands of police officers. According to the report,

> The youth, many of whom had been kicked out of their homes because of their sexual and gender identities, found themselves unemployable and forced to fall back on the sex trade as a source of income or shelter. "I understand that there are laws and there are people who don't always try to follow the laws," said one interviewee. "But when somebody is trying and you can see that it's a need, they just need to have some humanity. If you must arrest me for panhandling then understand that I didn't eat in three days."

LGBTQ-awareness trainings such as the ones Brian Sharp facilitates can go a long way toward building better relations between police departments and LGBTQ communities.

Chapter 5

FEDERAL OFFICERS

*T*here are a number of opportunities for police officers who want to work for a federal agency such as the Federal Bureau of Investigation, Drug Enforcement Administration, Department of Homeland Security, and others. These positions typically require a bachelor's degree and at least three years of related work experience. Once agents are hired, they will go through several weeks of specialized training with their agency. Most federal agents are trained at either the US Marine Corps base in Quantico, Virginia, or the Federal Law Enforcement Training Center in Glynco, Georgia.

FEDERAL BUREAU OF INVESTIGATION

The Federal Bureau of Investigation (FBI) is the government's main investigative department. An FBI agent's job is to protect the country from terrorist attacks, cyber (computer)

 This building is the FBI headquarters in Washington, DC. There are fifty-six field offices in cities across the country, hundreds of resident agencies in smaller cities, and over sixty offices in other countries.

attacks, organized crime, and violent crimes. Some of the crimes the FBI may look into include money laundering, kidnapping, drug trafficking, bank robbery, terrorism, foreign spying, and civil rights abuses.

The FBI has been in existence for more than one hundred years. The organization is based in Washington, DC, but it has fifty-six field offices in big cities across the United States, about four hundred resident agencies in smaller US cities, and more than sixty offices around the world.

Media Myths about FBI Agents

There are so many TV shows and movies about FBI agents that many people think they already know what the job entails. However, many of the scenarios that are portrayed in the media are exaggerated for entertainment value. Gary Noesner served in the FBI for thirty years as an investigator, instructor, and negotiator. In an interview with Business Insider, he dispelled some common myths about the work of an FBI agent:

> The public believes the FBI is spying on everyone, knows everything, has these abilities to gather any and all information. Popular shows like *CSI* are nice and entertaining, but they do *not* reflect reality.
>
> Also, people think the FBI is so secretive. There's only a very small amount of information that an FBI agent would not be able to share with someone. Unless something or someone is under investigation, we can usually talk about what we're working on or have worked on in the past.
>
> The biggest myth of all is that the FBI comes in and tells the cops to "get the hell out," like they do on TV and in movies. Sometimes the FBI can be arrogant, but that is so overplayed in Hollywood. There is typically a cooperative interaction where the FBI works closely with the police, shares information, and that is rarely shown on TV.

Working for the FBI can be very exciting. One week, an agent may be interviewing sources to gather evidence for a terrorism case, and the next week he or she may be trailing a suspected Mafia boss. However, it is more difficult to land a job with the FBI than with a local police force. Applicants must hold a college degree and have at least three years of professional work experience, or they must have an advanced degree, such as a master's degree, and two years of professional work experience. It is helpful for agents to have majored in an area such as computer science, information technology, a foreign language, or law.

Before being considered for a job with the FBI, applicants must go through a very thorough background check to make sure they do not have a criminal past. After getting hired, all FBI agents do approximately twenty weeks of training at the FBI Academy on the US Marine Corps base in Quantico, Virginia.

DRUG ENFORCEMENT ADMINISTRATION

US Drug Enforcement Administration (DEA) agents oversee and enforce federal laws that relate to controlled and illegal substances, particularly those involving narcotics and other unsafe drugs. They arrest and prosecute people who grow, make, sell, or distribute illegal drugs or who are involved in violence related to drugs. DEA agents may go undercover or travel to other countries to monitor and shut down illegal drug organizations.

DEA agents must be at least twenty-one years old but no older than thirty-six. They should be a US citizen and hold a college degree. Special consideration is given to those who hold degrees in criminal justice or police science. They need to have graduated with at least a 2.95 grade point average (about a B minus). Otherwise, they should have one year of experience conducting criminal investigations, three years of work experience plus special skills (such as those required for a pilot, accountant, or

DEA officers uphold laws relating to the trade of illegal substances. On April 16, 2018, US and Canadian officers seized a record amount of cocaine while patrolling the Eastern Pacific.

linguist), or a law degree. The application process can take up to a year. It includes a qualifications review, written test, panel interview, medical exam, physical test, lie detector test, psychological test, and background investigation. A drug test is one of the most important parts of the application process. For obvious reasons, the DEA does not want to hire special agents who are using illegal drugs.

Once hired, new DEA agents must go through eighteen weeks of training at the DEA Training Academy on the

Marine Corps base at Quantico, Virginia. There, they learn skills such as defense tactics, intelligence gathering, and use of firearms.

BUREAU OF ALCOHOL, TOBACCO, FIREARMS, AND EXPLOSIVES

The Bureau of Alcohol, Tobacco, Firearms, and Explosives (ATF) is a law enforcement agency within the US Department of Justice that protects the public from violent crimes. Its agents investigate crimes related to firearms, explosives, alcohol, and tobacco. An ATF agent may perform surveillance, conduct raids of suspects' homes or businesses, and prepare evidence to present in court.

To get a job with the ATF, applicants must be at least twenty-one years old and hold a college degree. Once they are hired, they must go through training at the Federal Law Enforcement Training Center in Glynco, Georgia. There, they learn about surveillance, arrest techniques, firearms use, and explosives investigation.

US SECRET SERVICE

The US Secret Service was created in the 1800s. Back then, its job was to prevent criminals from producing and using counterfeit money. The agency still has these duties. It also safeguards the country's financial and payment system. Its main responsibility today, however, is to protect national leaders, including the US president, visiting heads of state, the US vice president, and their families. Secret Service agents are the men and women who, if necessary, will place their own body in the path of an assassin's bullet to save the president's life.

To become a Secret Service agent, a person must be between twenty-one and thirty-seven years old. He or she must have graduated from college in the top third of the class or have one year of experience working in a law enforcement or investigative position. The application process involves a physical fitness evaluation, written test, and interviews. Applicants must get top-secret clearance by passing a lie detector test, drug screening, and a thorough background check.

DEPARTMENT OF HOMELAND SECURITY

Following the September 11, 2001, terrorist attacks on the World Trade Center in New York City and the Pentagon outside Washington, DC, the US Department of Homeland Security (DHS) was established by Congress and the president in 2002 to prevent terrorist attacks and aid in recovery efforts should another attack occur. Protecting the country from terrorism involves patrolling public transit systems, landmarks, ports, and power plants; increasing security at major events, such as Fourth of July celebrations; and securing the nation's borders to prevent terrorists from sneaking into the United States.

The US Customs and Border Protection, a division within the DHS, includes uniformed men and women who make up the biggest law enforcement group in the country. Border Patrol agents, for example, must be US citizens, and they should be under the age of thirty-seven when they are hired. They must have a bachelor's degree or previous related experience (for example, as a police officer), and pass an exam that evaluates their language and reasoning skills.

The Transportation Security Administration (TSA) is part of the Department of Homeland Security (DHS), which was established in 2002 to prevent terrorist attacks.

A number of other jobs are available within the DHS, including US Immigration and Customs Enforcement Special Agent, US Secret Service agent, and US Coast Guard officer. Each of these agencies within the DHS has its own job requirements. People who are interested in a career with the DHS can check directly with the organization for individual job descriptions.

FEDERAL AIR MARSHAL SERVICE

Federal air marshals in the Federal Air Marshal Service work for the Transportation Security Administration (TSA), which is part of the DHS. Their job is to protect the security of airline passengers. The United States first started its sky marshal program in 1970, following the hijacking of several commercial airplanes. After terrorists flew planes into the World Trade Center and Pentagon on September 11, 2001, security in the air became a top priority and the program was expanded.

Federal air marshals work in airports and fly on selected commercial flights. They don't wear uniforms because they must look like the other passengers. If trouble occurs on a flight, they use their specialized training in firearms and self-defense to keep the passengers safe. Federal air marshals must be US citizens, younger than thirty-seven at the time of appointment, and have at least three years of experience in law enforcement, security, or another professional field.

US MARSHALS SERVICE

The US Marshals Service is the oldest law enforcement agency in the United States. It has been in existence since 1789, and it still plays a very important role in the criminal justice system. The program includes ninety-four US marshals (one for each federal court district) and more than three thousand deputy US marshals and criminal investigators. Deputy US marshals have the following responsibilities:

◘ Bringing in fugitives who are wanted for federal crimes
◘ Protecting judges and jurors during federal court cases
◘ Running the Witness Security Program, which protects people whose lives may be in jeopardy after they testify against dangerous criminals
◘ Transporting federal prisoners
◘ Retrieving property that has been acquired by criminals through illegal activities

Requirements for US marshals are similar to those of other federal law enforcement positions. Applicants must be between the ages of twenty-one and thirty-six. They must have a four-year college degree, three years of related work experience, or a combination of education and work experience. After being hired, recruits have to complete a twenty-one-and-a-half week basic-training program in Glynco, Georgia.

Chapter 6

THE FUTURE OF POLICING

According to 2018 data from the Bureau of Labor Statistics, employment of police officers and detectives was projected to grow by 7 percent between 2016 and 2026, which is average for most occupations. Despite falling crime rates, there is expected to be a continued demand for police officers to maintain and improve public safety. The field is likely to remain competitive because of low job turnover, but those with a bachelor's degree or experience in law enforcement or the military will have the best chances of being hired. Job opportunities vary from place to place and from year to year because the level of employment is determined by the amount of government funding.

Competition for jobs at state and federal agencies is tougher because the salaries are generally higher. As a

Future job prospects for police officers look good. Some types of jobs in the police force are more competitive than others, but there will always be jobs for those who are willing to work hard.

result, the demand for jobs in state and federal departments is greater than the number of jobs available, and these departments can be very selective about which candidates they hire.

PROS AND CONS OF BEING A POLICE OFFICER

Working as a police officer can be very rewarding. One of the biggest advantages is the excitement that comes with the job. For those who crave adventure, this is an ideal career. Author Stephanie Watson interviewed a number of police officers about the pros and cons of being a part of the police force.

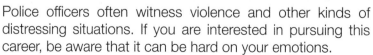

Police officers often witness violence and other kinds of distressing situations. If you are interested in pursuing this career, be aware that it can be hard on your emotions.

"After twenty-seven-plus years, I still enjoy my job," said Robin Matthews, an inspector (detective) with the San Francisco Police Department. "I grew up wanting to be a police officer since I was a young child, and it didn't disappoint me. It never got boring, and every day was different."

Working in a job that involves saving lives can be especially satisfying. A lot of respect and pride comes from wearing a police officer's uniform. "At the end of the day, I'm thankful and very proud of my profession," said Jennifer McFeggan of the Hamilton Police Service in Ontario, Canada.

The field of law enforcement also involves many challenges. Being a police officer in real life is far different from how it is portrayed on television. Police officers are not always involved in car chases or shootouts. Much of the time, officers sit at their desks and fill out paperwork or patrol quiet streets. They may have to work long hours or stay outside in cold or stormy weather.

Often, even an officer's best efforts cannot bring criminals to justice. It can be frustrating for officers to learn that they worked hard to arrest a suspect, only to be told that the court system released that person without requiring them to serve any jail time.

One of the most difficult issues for officers to deal with is the loss of life that can occur on their watch. For FBI agents like Jesse Maddox, knowing that someone he was trying to protect has died is really difficult, especially when the crime involves a child. "It just plays over and over in your head," he said. "You can't stay totally emotionless because you wouldn't have any passion for your job, but you do need to stay detached."

HOURS AND BENEFITS

Although law enforcement isn't a traditional nine-to-five job (it's common to work nights, weekends, and holidays— especially for junior officers), the hours are reasonable. Most police officers and detectives work at least a forty-hour week. Sometimes when they are working on a particularly difficult investigation, officers and detectives

It's important for police officers to build and maintain strong relationships with the communities they serve. These human connections can make the job highly rewarding.

will have to work overtime. In those situations, officers will receive extra pay (usually their full hourly pay rate, plus half of that rate).

Police officers get excellent benefits, which include paid vacation, sick leave, health and life insurance, and sometimes college tuition assistance. People in most professions have to wait until they are sixty-five or seventy years old to retire and receive their pensions. Police officers, however, have the option to retire early with benefits. Depending on when they started working for their police department, some officers are young enough when they retire to start a new career.

The Evolution of Policing in America

Over the decades, the ways that the police force operates in the United States has changed in response to a number of significant events. According to Darrell Stephens, executive director of Major Cities Chiefs Association, the attack on the World Trade Center on September 11, 2001, had a major impact on policing across the country. "Before 9/11, we spent a lot of work developing relationships and problem-solving, which led to positive connections in most of our communities. 9/11 caused a shift in the way folks focused on resources, particularly in larger urban areas."

One of these shifts was a vast increase in funding for state and local law enforcement agencies, which led to police in

(continued on the next page)

(continued from the previous page)

many areas being armed with military-style weapons and heavily armored vehicles. Many people across the country became aware of the militarization of police as a problem after the fatal shooting of unarmed black teenager Michael Brown in Ferguson, Missouri, on August 9, 2014, when local police responded to protesters with military weapons and armored vehicles.

Joe Schafer, president of the Society of Police Futurists International, said in an interview with PoliceOne.com that the events in Ferguson contributed to another shift in policing, helping people to realize that "policing is still the most effective when it is done *with* people, not *to* people. We may have forgotten that a little bit in the 2000s, where policing became something done *to* communities rather than with communities. Ferguson may have been one of the more positive outcomes, reminding us that those local connections and relationships matter." Schafer went on to say that it's important to hold on to the human aspects of policing and to maintain strong relationships between police officers and the communities they are serving.

THE FUTURE JOB OUTLOOK IN LAW ENFORCEMENT

No job is completely recession proof—even a job in law enforcement. The number of police jobs is based on how much money local, state, and federal governments have available to spend on their police forces. That amount can vary from year to year. If government budgets get trimmed, law enforcement jobs can be cut as well.

Overall, though, law enforcement remains an exciting, meaningful, and profitable profession. For people who pursue a career as a police officer or one of the many other jobs available in the field, there are still plenty of opportunities. Police officers enjoy good salaries, excellent benefits, and the satisfaction that comes from saving lives and making a real difference in their communities.

Glossary

CITATION Official documentation stating that a person has committed a violation; also called a ticket.

CYBER CRIME A criminal act carried out using computers or the internet.

DETECTIVE A police officer who investigates crimes and gathers evidence relating to criminal activity.

FEDERAL AIR MARSHAL A federal officer who protects airline passengers.

FELONY A crime that is considered more serious than a misdemeanor and is typically punishable by imprisonment of at least one year or the death penalty.

FORENSICS The use of science in criminal investigation.

FUGITIVE A person involved in a criminal case who tries to hide from law enforcement officials.

HOSTAGE A person who is taken by force and held as a means of securing the taker's demands.

K-9 OFFICER A police officer who works with dogs; also called a handler.

LIEUTENANT A law enforcement officer who is ranked above police sergeant and has leadership responsibilities.

MILITIA An organization of nonprofessional fighters.

MIRANDA RIGHTS A notification given by police officers to criminal suspects, informing them of their right to silence and to counsel.

MOUNTED OFFICER A police officer who rides a horse.

PATROL OFFICER A uniformed police officer who works for state or local law enforcement and typically enforces laws and responds to emergencies in a specific geographical area.

POLICE CORPORAL A law enforcement officer ranked above police officer and below police sergeant.

POLICE SERGEANT A law enforcement officer ranked above police corporal and below police lieutenant.

ROOKIE Someone who is new to the job.

SEX WORKERS People who trade sexual services for money, goods, or services.

SHERIFF A law enforcement official who works for a county or city and is usually elected to the position.

STATE POLICE OFFICER A police officer who works for the state; also called a state trooper.

SURVEILLANCE A means of monitoring people in order to gather information.

TASER A brand of weapon that delivers an electric shock and is used to cause temporary paralysis.

TRAFFIC OFFICER A uniformed officer who patrols the roads and highways enforcing traffic laws; also known as a highway patrol officer.

TRANS Short for transgender; people whose gender identity is different from their biological sex.

TRANSIT AUTHORITY OFFICER A police officer who is assigned to patrol the subway in a big city.

WARRANT Official documentation issued by a judge or magistrate, authorizing the arrest of a person or search of a property.

For More Information

Blacks in Law Enforcement of America (BLEA)
405 Tarrytown Road, #1318
White Plains, NY 10607
(914) 525-5288
Website: https://www.bleausa.org
Facebook and Twitter: @BLEAUSA
BLEA is an organization of police officers of color
working to ensure equality in policing. It provides
community support and trainings that promote a
cooperative partnership between police and people
of color and create safer communities.

Bureau of Labor Statistics
Postal Square Building, 2 Massachusetts Avenue NE
Washington, DC 20212
(202) 691-5200
Website: https://www.bls.gov/home.htm
Twitter: @BLS_gov
The Bureau of Labor Statistics provides comprehensive
information and statistics about all types of labor,
including the qualifications required for a profession
and links to additional job information resources.

Canadian Association of Chiefs of Police (CACP)
300 Terry Fox Drive, Unit 100
Kanata, ON K2K 0E3
Canada
(613) 595-1101
Website: https://www.cacp.ca/index.html
Twitter: @CACP_ACCP

The CACP is a political lobbying organization that
advocates for police professionals across Canada.

Canadian Police Association (CPA)
Suite 100, 141 Catherine Street
Ottawa, ON K2P 1C3
Canada
(613) 231-4168
Website: https://www.cpa-acp.ca
Facebook: @CanadianPoliceAssociation
The CPA is a membership organization serving police
professionals across Canada. The organization
provides advocacy, education, and resources.

Federal Criminal Investigators Association (FCIA)
PO Box 23400
Washington, DC 20026
(630) 969-8537
Website: http://www.fedcia.org
FCIA provides education, advocacy, and support for
professionals in the federal investigative community.

Federal Law Enforcement Officers Association (FLEOA)
1100 Connecticut Avenue NW, Suite 900
Washington, DC 20036
(202) 293-1550
Website: https://www.fleoa.org/default.aspx
Facebook:
    @Federal-Law-Enforcement-Officers-Association
Twitter: @FLEOAORG

FLEOA is a nonprofit membership organization offering legal assistance and advocacy for federal law enforcement officers.

International Association of Chiefs of Police (IACP)
44 Canal Center Plaza, #200
Alexandria, VA 22314
(703) 836-6767
Website: https://www.theiacp.org
Facebook and Twitter: @TheIACP
The IACP is a professional association representing police leaders from all over the world. It is the publisher of *The Police Chief* magazine and the organizer of the IACP Annual Conference.

International Association of Women Police (IAWP)
12600 Kavanaugh Lane
Bowie, MD 20715
Website: https://iawppublic.wildapricot.org
Twitter: @IAWPinfo
The IAWP is a global organization for women in the police force. Its mission is to raise awareness of the importance of women in the police force and provide support and events for female police officers.

National Association of Police Organizations (NAPO)
317 South Patrick Street
Alexandria, VA 22314
(703) 549-0775
Website: http://www.napo.org

Facebook: @National-Association-of-Police
    -Organizations-NAPO
Twitter: @NAPOpolice
NAPO is a coalition of police unions and associations
    providing advocacy and education to its members
    across the United States.

National Sheriffs' Association (NSA)
1450 Duke Street
Alexandria, VA 22314
(800) 424-7827
Website: https://www.sheriffs.org
Facebook: @NationalSheriffAssociation
Twitter: @NationalSheriff
The NSA is a professional association representing
    sheriffs, deputies, and other law enforcement
    professionals. It provides training, informational
    resources, and other services.

For Further Reading

Bickerstaff, Linda. *Careers in Undercover Narcotics Investigation.* New York, NY: Rosen Publishing, 2014.

Brezina, Corona. *Careers in the Homicide Unit.* New York, NY: Rosen Publishing, 2014.

Fitzgerald, Lee. *Mounted and Canine Police.* New York, NY: Rosen Publishing, 2016.

Grinapol, Corinne. *Careers on Antiterrorism and Counterterrorism Task Forces.* New York, NY: Rosen Publishing, 2014.

Johnston, Coy H. *Careers in Law Enforcement.* Los Angeles, CA: SAGE, 2017.

La Bella, Laura. *Careers in Crisis Management and Hostage Negotiation.* New York, NY: Rosen Publishing, 2014.

Mullenbach, Cheryl. *Women in Blue: 16 Brave Officers, Forensic Experts, Police Chiefs, and More.* Chicago, IL: Chicago Review Press, 2016.

Porterfield, Jason. *Careers in Undercover Gang Investigation.* New York, NY: Rosen Publishing, 2014.

Schroeder, Donald J., and Frank A. Lombardo. *Police Officer Exam.* Hauppage, NY: Barron's, 2017.

Suen, Anastasia. *Careers with SWAT Teams.* New York, NY: Rosen Publishing, 2014.

Bibliography

Adams, Eric L. "We Must Stop Police Abuse of Black Men." *New York Times*, December 4, 2014. https://www.nytimes.com/2014/12/05/opinion/we-must-stop-police-abuse-of-black-men.html.

Bekiempis, Victoria. "Meet the Cop Who Wants to Fix LGBT-Police Relations." *Newsweek*, October 24, 2018. https://www.newsweek.com/police-officer-improve-cop-lgbt-relations-380468.

Bureau of Labor Statistics. "Police and Detectives." Retrieved October 23, 2018. https://www.bls.gov/ooh/protective-service/police-and-detectives.htm.

Career Profiles. "Police Officer." Retrieved December 3, 2018. http://www.careerprofiles.info/police-officer.html.

Criminal Justice Degree Schools. "Police Officer: Career Guide." Retrieved December 3, 2018. https://www.criminaljusticedegreeschools.com/criminal-justice-careers/police-officer.

Criminal Justice USA. "How to Become a Police Officer." Retrieved December 3, 2018. https://www.criminaljusticeusa.com/police-officer.

Dank, Meredith, et al. "Locked In: Interactions with the Criminal Justice and Child Welfare Systems for LGBTQ Youth, YMSM, and YWSW Who Engage in Survival Sex." Urban Institute, September 29, 2015. https://www.urban.org/research/publication/locked-interactions-criminal-justice-and-child-welfare-systems-lgbtq-youth-ymsm-and-ywsw-who-engage-survival-sex.

Dees, Tim. "What Is It Like After You Graduate the Police Academy and Become a Real Cop?" Slate, October 11, 2013. https://slate.com/human

-interest/2013/10/police-officers-what-is-it-like-to
-be-a-rookie-cop.html.

De Sturler, Alice. "National Police Week 2011: Suzie
Ivy." Defrosting Cold Cases, May 15, 2011. https://
defrostingcoldcases.com/national-police-week
-2011-suzie-ivy.

Dr. Kit Career Videos. "K-9 Police Officer, Career
Video." January 24, 2012. https://www.youtube
.com/watch?v=sWZPoa-KymQ.

Hawk, Christopher. "What's It Really Like to Be a Cop?"
HuffPost, November 12, 2015. https://www
.huffingtonpost.com/quora/what-its-really-like-to
-b_b_8545514.html.

Hayasaki, Erika. "Life of a Police Officer." *The Atlantic*,
March 14, 2014. https://www.theatlantic.com/health
/archive/2014/03/life-of-a-police-officer-medically
-and-psychologically-ruinous/284324.

How to Become a Police Officer. "Interview with
Suzie Ivy, Police Detective and Author of *Bad Luck
Detective*." Retrieved October 23, 2018. https://
www.how-to-become-a-police-officer.com/expert
-advice/suzy-ivy.

Learn How to Become. "Law Enforcement Degrees
and Police Careers." Retrieved October 23, 2018.
https://www.learnhowtobecome.org/police-officer.

Maddox, Jesse. Assistant Special Agent in Charge,
Georgia Bureau of Investigation. Interview with
Stephanie Watson, July 13, 2009.

Matthews, Robin. Inspector, San Francisco Police
Department, CA. Interview with Stephanie Watson,
July 6, 2009.

McFeggan, Jennifer. Senior Constable, Hamilton Police Service. Interview with Stephanie Watson, July 14, 2009.

National Association of Police Organizations. "About NAPO." Retrieved October 23, 2018. http://www.napo.org.

National Public Radio. "Why a Black Teen Who Was Beaten by Police Decided to Join the NYPD." *Fresh Air*, July 21, 2016. https://www.npr.org/2016/07/21/486892032/an-african-american-police-officer-on-his-choice-to-be-a-voice-for-change.

Perry, Nancy. "Looking Back, Looking Forward: Predicting the State of Policing in 2043." PoliceOne.com, June 22, 2018. https://www.policeone.com/police-products/body-cameras/articles/476842006-LooErikaking-back-looking-forward-Predicting-the-state-of-policing-in-2043.

Police Tutorial Service. "Actual Examination Practice Questions: Lieutenant/Captain Examination." Retrieved October 23, 2018. https://www.policetutorialservice.com/sample.php?catid=4.

Princeton Review, The. "A Day in the Life of a Police Officer/Manager." Retrieved December 3, 2018. https://www.princetonreview.com/careers/120/police-officer-manager.

Roufa, Timothy. "Learn About Becoming a Police Officer." The Balance Careers, August 15, 2018. https://www.thebalancecareers.com/becoming-a-police-officer-974896.

Roufa, Timothy. "The 10 Best Things About Being a
    Police Officer." The Balance Careers, September 8,
    2018. https://www.thebalancecareers.com/the-10
    -best-things-about-being-a-police-officer-974910.
Roufa, Timothy. "The 10 Worst Things About Being a
    Police Officer." The Balance Careers, October 2,
    2018. https://www.thebalancecareers.com/the-10
    -worst-things-about-being-a-police-officer-974911.
Smith, Jacquelyn. "Here's What It's Really Like to Work
    for the FBI." *Business Insider*, April 29, 2015. https://
    www.businessinsider.com/what-its-really-like-to
    -work-for-the-fbi-2015-4.

Index

A
Adams, Eric L., 8, 15–16
advancement, 27–29
arrests, 12
Atlanta Police Department (ABD), 46–47

B
background checks, 17, 18, 21–22
Blacks in Law Enforcement of America, 15
board interview, 22
bomb squad, 35
Border Patrol, 54
Brown, Michael, 64
Bureau of Alcohol, Tobacco, Firearms, and Explosives (ATF), 53
Bureau of Labor Statistics, 58

C
cadets, 16
certifications, 27
citizenship, 16
Coast Guard, 55
Customs and Border Protection, 54
cybercrime, 14, 48

D
Department of Homeland Security (DHS), 54–56
Department of Justice, 53
detectives, 40–44
Drug Enforcement Administration (DEA), 51–53

E
education, 13–15, 18, 24, 28–30, 34, 39, 43, 51, 53, 54, 57
election, 39

F
Federal Air Marshal Service, 56
Federal Bureau of Investigation (FBI), 9, 48–51, 61
Federal Law Enforcement Training Center, 48, 53
felony, 17, 36
Ferguson, Missouri, 64
field training officer (FTO), 27
fish and game, 45
forensics, 14, 40
fugitive, 45, 57
fugitive search, 45

G
Glynco, Georgia, 48, 53, 57
Gross, Terri, 8

H
Hamilton Police Service, 61
harbor patrol, 45
hostage, 45

I
Immigration and Customs
    Enforcement, 55
interns, 16
investigation, 12
Ivy, Suzie, 6–8, 43–44

J
job prospects, 58–59
juvenile officer, 45

K
K-9 officers, 35–37

L
LGBTQ communities,
    46–47

M
Maddox, Jesse, 61

Marshals Service, 56–57
Matthews, Robin, 61
McFeggan, Jennifer, 61
media portrayals, 50
militia, 14
Miranda rights, 12
mounted police, 35–36

N
National Association of
    Black Police Officers, 15
National Place Police
    Association, 15
New York Police
    Department (NYPD),
    15–16
911, 32
Noesner, Gary, 50

O
100 Blacks in Law
    Enforcement Who
    Care, 16
organized crime, 49

P
patrol officers, 32
Pensacola Police
    Department, 36
people of color, 15–16

ABOUT THE AUTHORS

Rachel Given-Wilson has written and edited a number of nonfiction books for teenagers, including the Tech Girls series of books about careers for girls in STEM industries. She lives in Brooklyn with her family.

Stephanie Watson is a writer and editor based in Atlanta, Georgia. She has written or contributed to numerous books, including *Anderson Cooper: Profile of a TV Journalist* and *How to Break in as a Television Producer.* She is a regular contributor of career reports to the Institute for Career Research, which provides vocational guidance information for young adults.

PHOTO CREDITS

Cover John Roman Images; back cover, pp. 6, 15, 16, 25, 26, 36, 37, 43, 44, 50, 63, 64 Fer Gregory/Shutterstock.com; p. 7 (inset) Jose Luis Pelaez Inc/Blend Images/Getty Images; p. 10 Photo Researchers /Science Source/Getty Images; p. 11 Jeremy Woodhouse/Blend Images/Getty Images; p. 14 Bob Daemmrich/Alamy Stock Photo; p. 20 Joe Amon/Denver Post/Getty Images; p. 23 Mario Tama /Getty Images; p. 28 Paul Zimmerman/Getty Images; p. 31 Leonard Zhukovsky/Shutterstock.com; p. 33 MCCAIG/E+/Getty Images; p. 37 George Frey/AFP/Getty Images; p. 38 Sandy Huffaker /Corbis News/Getty Images; p. 41 Kevin Curtis/Science Photo Library /Getty Images; p. 42 VStock LLC/Tanya Constantine/Getty Images; p. 45 Portland Press Herald/Getty Images; p. 49 Library of Congress Prints and Photographs Division; p. 52 Sandy Huffaker/Getty Images; p. 55 Bloomberg/Getty Images; p. 59 Stephanie Keith/Getty Images; p. 60 Mark Boster/Los Angeles Times/Getty Images; p. 62 Nic Neufeld/Shutterstock.com.

Design and Layout: Nicole Russo-Duca; Photo Researcher: Sherri Jackson

A Note to Parents and Teachers

DK READERS is a compelling program for beginning readers, designed in conjunction with leading literacy experts, including Dr. Linda Gambrell, director of the Eugene T. Moore School of Education, Clemson University, and past president of the National Reading Conference.

Beautiful illustrations and superb full-color photographs combine with engaging, easy-to-read stories to offer a fresh approach to each subject in the series. Each DK READER is guaranteed to capture a child's interest while developing his or her reading skills, general knowledge, and love of reading.

The four levels of DK READERS are aimed at different reading abilities, enabling you to choose the books that are exactly right for your children:

Level 1 – Beginning to read
Level 2 – Beginning to read alone
Level 3 – Reading alone
Level 4 – Proficient readers

The "normal" age at which a child begins to read can be anywhere from three to eight years old, so these levels are only a general guideline.

No matter which level you select, you can be sure that you are helping your child learn to read, then read to learn!

LONDON, NEW YORK, MELBOURNE,
MUNICH, AND DELHI

Senior Editor Beth Sutinis
Senior Art Editor Michelle Baxter
Publisher Chuck Lang
Creative Director Tina Vaughan
Production Chris Avgherinos
DTP Designer Milos Orlovic

Reading Consultant
Linda Gambrell, Ph.D.

Produced by
Shoreline Publishing Group LLC
Editorial Director James Buckley, Jr.
Art Director Tom Carling
Carling Design, Inc.

First American Edition, 2004

04 05 06 10 9 8 7 6 5 4 3 2 1
Published in the United States by DK Publishing, Inc.
375 Hudson St., New York, New York 10014

Copyright © 2004 DK Publishing, Inc.
All rights reserved under International and Pan-American Copyright
Conventions. No part of this publication may be reproduced, stored
in a retrieval system, or transmitted in any form or by any means,
electronic, mechanical, photocopying, recording, or otherwise, without
the prior written permission of the copyright owner.

Published in Great Britain by Dorling Kindersley Limited.

ISBN: 0-7894-9898-7 (PB)
ISBN: 0-7894-9897-9 (HC)

A Catalog Record is available from the Library of Congress.

Color reproduction by Colourscan, Singapore
Printed and bound in Belgium by Proost

Photography credits:
t=top, b=below, l=left, r=right, c=center
AFP/Corbis: 10; Bettmann/Corbis: 5, 6, 7; Brand X Pictures: 5t;
Caron/Corbis Sygma: 12t; Duomo/Corbis: 8, 9, 14, 20, 21, 29, 30t,
31; Jeff Kowalsky/Corbis Sygma: 17; Wally McNamee/Corbis: 12b,
16, 19; Mug Shots/Corbis: 30b; Reuters NewMedia/Corbis: 13, 15t,
18, 22, 23, 25, 26, 28; Robert Siemoneit/Corbis Sygma: 11; Tim
Thompson/Corbis: 27; Underwood & Underwood/Corbis: 4; Karl
Weatherly/Corbis: 15b.

Discover more at
www.dk.com

AP 28TH

READERS

BEGINNING TO READ ALONE 2

Ice Skating Stars

BEGINNING
READER
J796.912
BUC

Written by James Buckley, Jr.

DK

BARRINGTON AREA LIBRARY
505 N. NORTHWEST HWY.
BARRINGTON, ILLINOIS 60010

Sonja Henie was the first great ice skating star.

As music fills the ice skating arena, the skater glides, dances, and spins. She combines strength, style, and grace. To many fans, skating is one of the world's most beautiful sports. This book tells the story of the greatest ice skating stars.

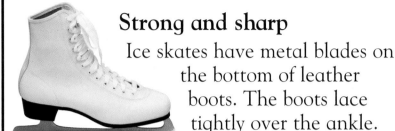

Strong and sharp
Ice skates have metal blades on the bottom of leather boots. The boots lace tightly over the ankle.

Norway's Sonja Henie (SOHN-ya HENN-ee) set the stage for future stars. She was in her first Olympics at age 11. After she won gold medals in 1928, 1932, and 1936, she skated in movies.

Henie wore bright and colorful outfits while skating.

Tenley Albright sharpened her skates before skating for Olympic gold.

Skating became one of the most popular Winter Olympics events. Every four years, athletes gather to compete in these Winter Games. In 1956, Tenley Albright became the first American woman to win the Olympic gold medal.

Peggy Fleming, who was born in California, won the gold medal in 1968. Peggy won because of her smooth and elegant style.

Peggy Fleming was pretty in pink in 1968.

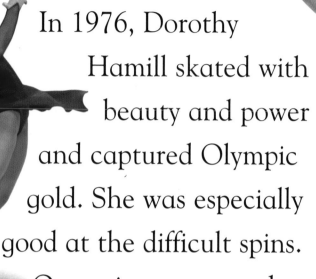

In 1976, Dorothy Hamill skated with beauty and power and captured Olympic gold. She was especially good at the difficult spins. One spin was named after Dorothy. It is called the Hamill Camel.
After the Olympics, she became a popular star of skating shows.

Men skate, too!
This book features the best female skaters. Men are also wonderful and talented skaters.

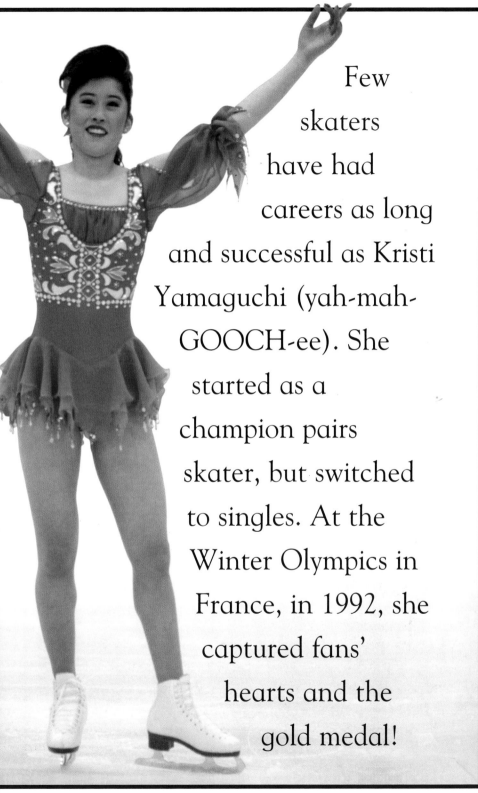

Few skaters have had careers as long and successful as Kristi Yamaguchi (yah-mah-GOOCH-ee). She started as a champion pairs skater, but switched to singles. At the Winter Olympics in France, in 1992, she captured fans' hearts and the gold medal!

Not all ice skating stars come from the United States. In 1984 and 1988, a woman from East Germany became the first since Sonja Henie to win two gold medals in a row.

Katarina Witt thrilled fans with her powerful skating style. After her Olympic

Katarina Witt

success, she danced and skated in movies and became a model. She also worked as a skating announcer on television.

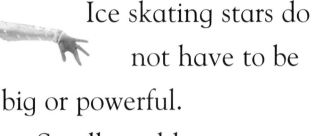

Ice skating stars do not have to be big or powerful. Smaller athletes can do very well. One example is Oksana Baiul (by-YOOL). Though not even five feet (1.65 m) tall, she was a giant of skating. In 1994, she leaped, twirled, and spun to Olympic gold.

Oksana cried when she saw her winning score.

Still tearful, Oksana waved to the crowd after getting her gold medal.

Like many skaters in recent years, Oksana was a success while young. She was only 16 years old when she became an Olympic ice skating champion.

Irina shows that skaters must be very flexible.

Skaters must train very hard for years. Often they can take a long time to make it to the top. Many never do. Russian skater Irina Slutskaya probably thought her time would not come.

Here is the happy smile of a skating champion!

She had won four European Figure Skating Championships.
She had won a silver medal (second place) at the Olympics.
Finally, in 2002, Irina's many years of hard work paid off. She won the World Championship!

Two on the ice
Men and women team up to skate in pairs. They skate together to music and perform special routines.

American skaters continue to be among the world's best. One skater captured the hearts of millions of fans with her athletic moves.

Tara Lipinski

Tara Lipinski was only 14 years old when she was the surprise winner of the 1997 World Championship while landing seven "triples." In a triple axel, a skater leaps in the air and spins three and one half times before landing cleanly.

Heading into the 1998 Winter Olympics in Japan, few experts thought Tara could win.

She was only 15 years old, and would have to beat many experienced skaters.

But Tara did it!

She became the youngest Winter Olympic gold medalist ever!

Fiery honor

In 2002, Tara Lipinski took part in the Olympic torch relay. The flame on the torch helped start the Winter Games in Utah.

After her Olympic win, Tara went on to win the 1999 World Championship.

Tara was a happy gold medal winner.

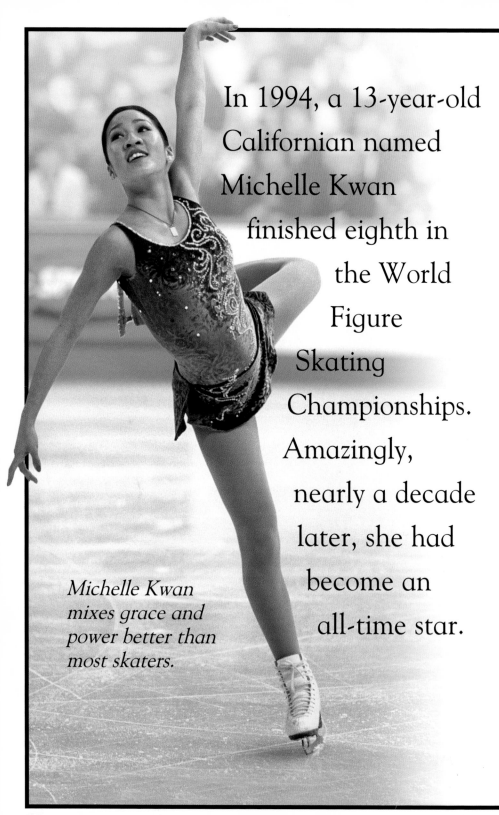

In 1994, a 13-year-old Californian named Michelle Kwan finished eighth in the World Figure Skating Championships. Amazingly, nearly a decade later, she had become an all-time star.

Michelle Kwan mixes grace and power better than most skaters.

Michelle has had one of the greatest careers of any skating star. She has been the U.S. champion seven times, and she has won five world championships.
She has not won a gold medal in the Olympics, however. In 1998, she won a silver medal, and in 2002, she won a bronze (third place). But her bright smile and great talent have made her a favorite of millions of fans.

Michelle Kwan

Michelle really gets into her music!

While younger skaters have tried to challenge her, Michelle has stayed on top. She is a powerful skater.

She can leap and spin very well and is excellent at landing cleanly.

Michelle is also a great dancer. During her routines, she often has fans clapping along with the bouncy music.

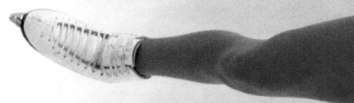

Few skaters in history have had as much success as Michelle, and few have been more beloved.

As Michelle shows here, skaters must be like gymnasts on ice.

Every four years, skating fans look forward to the Winter Olympics. The skating events are always among the most popular. Millions of people around the world watch on TV. Tickets to the events are always hard to get.

At these events, with everyone watching closely, a skater can suddenly become a superstar.

That happened to a young American skater in 2002. Sarah Hughes overcame more experienced skaters to win!

In the Olympics, skaters perform two routines. The short program comes first. It counts for one-third of a skater's final score.

In 2002, Sarah finished fourth in the short program. That made her chances for a medal very slim. In Olympic history, no skater had come from fourth place in the short program to win the gold medal.

On the ice
Skaters perform on large ice surfaces in special arenas called "rinks."

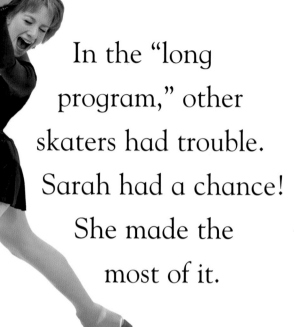

In the "long program," other skaters had trouble. Sarah had a chance! She made the most of it.

Skating with power, grace, and enthusiasm, Sarah thrilled the crowd and the judges.
Her routine was difficult to perform but exciting to watch.
She performed it beautifully. When the event was over, Sarah had won the gold medal!

Sarah later won the 2002 Sullivan Award, given to the top amateur athlete in the United States.

Sarah is also a great student. She now attends Yale University in Connecticut.

Sarah shows off her hard-earned gold medal.

From Sonja Henie to Sarah Hughes, skating stars have thrilled people for decades. Who will be the next ice skating stars?

Sasha Cohen

American skaters are sure to be among them. Sasha Cohen is one to watch. She was fourth at the 2002 Olympics and World Championships.

Learning to skate
All the skating stars in this book learned to skate while young with the help of coaches and parents.

Top skaters compete first in "junior" events. Beatrisa Liang (lee-YANG) is a recent U.S. junior champion. Will she one day grab Olympic gold? The road to the top of the skating world is a long one. But with hard work, maybe *you* can make it, too!

Beatrisa Liang

Olympic Gold Medalists

Here are the women who have won Olympic gold medals in individual figure skating.

Year	Skater, Country
1908	Madge Syers, Great Britain
1920	Magda Julin, Sweden
1924	Herma Szabo-Planck, Austria
1928	Sonja Henie, Norway
1932	Sonja Henie, Norway
1936	Sonja Henie, Norway
1948	Barbara Ann Scott, Canada
1952	Jeanette Altwegg, Great Britain
1956	Tenley Albright, United States
1960	Carol Heiss, United States
1964	Sjoukje Dijkstra, Netherlands
1968	Peggy Fleming, United States
1972	Beatrix Schuba, Austria
1976	Dorothy Hamill, United States
1980	Anett Potzsch, East Germany
1984	Katarina Witt, East Germany
1988	Katarina Witt, East Germany
1992	Kristi Yamaguchi, United States
1994	Oksana Baiul, Ukraine
1998	Tara Lipinski, United States
2002	Sarah Hughes, United States
2006	

Index